SPACE!

MERCURY

To all scientists who devote their work lives to expand our view of the universe.

Marshall Cavendish Benchmark
99 White Plains Road
Tarrytown, New York 10591
www.marshallcavendish.us

Library of Congress Cataloging-in-Publication Data
Colligan, L. H.
  Mercury / by L.H. Colligan.
      p. cm. -- (Space!)
  Summary: "Describes Mercury, including its history, its composition, and its role in the solar system"-- Provided by publisher.
  Includes bibliographical references and index.
  ISBN 978-07614-4239-4
  1. Mercury (Planet)--Juvenile literature. I. Title.
  QB611.C655 2010
  523.41--dc22   2008037278

Editor: Karen Ang
Publisher: Michelle Bisson
Art Director: Anahid Hamparian
Series design by Daniel Roode
Production by nSight, Inc.

Front cover: Detlev van Ravenswaay / Photo Researchers Inc.
Title page: *Mariner 10*
Photo research by Candlepants Incorporated
Front cover: Detlev van Ravenswaay / Photo Researchers Inc.
The photographs in this book are used by permission and through the courtesy of: *Corbis:* 1, 34, 38; Myron Jay Dorf, 7; Denis Scott, 10; Roger Ressmeyer, 27; NASA/Roger Ressmeyer, 35; George Steinmetz, 39; Carleton Bailie for Boeing/Handout/Reuters, 51. *Photo Researchers Inc.:* Mehau Kulyk, 4, 5; David A. Hardy, 11; John Chumack, 14; Royal Astronomical Society/SPL, 25; Shigemi Numazawa / Atlas Photo Bank, 28; USGS, 36; Christian Darkin, 40; Science Source, 42; Victor Habbick Visions, 43; Mark Garlick, 44, 56; NASA/JHU-APL/ASU/Carnegie Institution of Washington/SPL, 54; Chris Bjornberg, 58. *The Image Works:* Werner Foreman / Topham, 16, 17; Macduff Everton, 20; Science Museum/SSPL, 24. *Getty Images:* Tony Hallas, 19; D'Arco Editori, 29; 30, 31; Time & Life Pictures, 32. *Art Resource, NY:* Bildarchiv Preussischer Kulturbesitz, 21; Erich Lessing, 22. NASA: Johns Hopkins University Applied Physics Laboratory/Carnegie Institution of Washington, 46, 47, 48, 53, 55, 57. *AP Images:* 52. Illustration on page 13 by Mapping Specialists © Marshall Cavendish Corporation.
Printed in Malaysia
123456

CONTENTS

1

THE FORMATION OF PLANETS

The huge event that began more than thirteen billion years ago was loud, but no one heard it. It was bright, but no one saw it. It was hot, but no living creature felt the heat. There were no **stars**, **moons**, or **asteroids**. Neither solid nor gaseous **planets** had formed. Our **solar system** had not been born yet.

No forms of life—bacteria, insects, plants, humans, or other animals—experienced the mammoth expansion of hot, concentrated matter and energy that took place all those billions of years ago. It was as if a tiny, packed balloon that started out the size of a speck, began to expand and did not stop. The huge expansion released gases and dust that have been traveling in space ever since.

The Big Bang expansion gave birth to our universe of galaxies, stars, and planets.

THE BIG BANG

Billions of years later, humans developed many explanations for how objects in the sky came to be. Most scientists now call the beginning of this ancient expansion the Big Bang. They have tested many theories about what happened right after the Big Bang expansion began. Telescopes, spacecraft, cameras, and computers have captured and analyzed images of objects in space that support many early theories about the Big Bang.

Based on repeated tests, nearly all scientists support the idea that hot, dense energy and matter were packed into a pinpoint. They still do not know the source of the pinpoint or what caused this matter to begin expanding. They do know—from measurements and tests—that the hot, spreading energy sent a massive cloud of gas and dust through space. As it cooled, the gas in the huge floating cloud was mainly composed of two chemical elements, hydrogen and helium.

Then something happened in this enormous cloud. Hydrogen and helium clustered together in some places. Within those clusters, the first stars began to form. But these were not stars as people think of them today. At first, they did not twinkle or brighten the sky, and they were not yet hot enough to give off light. Gradually, though, these stars pulled in more hydrogen and more helium. Temperature and pressure soared within some gas clusters. The combination of gases, gravity, and increased pressure caused new, heavier chemicals to form. The stars began to release energy in the form of heat and light. They began to shine.

In this way, during the course of billions of years, countless new stars formed. Millions of stars grouped together to form **galaxies**. At the same time, those first, older stars began to die as they used up their energy and cooled down. Some did not die quietly. They collapsed into themselves with so much force that they set off new explosions called supernovas. These star explosions, along with the slower deaths of other stars, sent new gases and dust-like particles into space. The space that contained this matter came to be called the **universe**.

The Milky Way is Earth's neighborhood, and is made of gas, dust, planets, and stars. Its oldest star is almost as old as the universe.

Within the universe, some matter developed into stars composed of complex chemicals. Other matter formed around the stars. They became moons, rocks, asteroids, and planets. The stars' gravity caused these objects to revolve around the stars in different systems throughout the universe. One of these solar systems is ours. In this system, eight planets formed—Jupiter, Saturn, Uranus, Neptune, Earth, Venus, Mars, and Mercury.

The Big Mystery of the Big Bang

If no one was around to hear or see the Big Bang that started the universe, how do scientists know what happened more than 13 billion years ago? Like detectives reconstructing a scene they did not witness firsthand, these scientists use tools to search for and analyze clues that they find.

Using an advanced telescope in 1919, Edwin Hubble shook up the world of **astronomy**. He was the first **astronomer** to observe other galaxies beyond Earth's Milky Way. Not only that, Hubble noticed that all galaxies in space were rapidly moving away from one another. That is what happens after something explodes or expands. Hubble's discovery of an expanding universe, tested and proven many times since, laid the foundation of the Big Bang theory.

Astronomers also use other tools to test theories about the Big Bang. Objects in space have individual characteristics, such as different lengths, colors, and chemical compositions. Scientists study these characteristics to identify the age, size, location, and composition of objects in space. Spectroscopes measure light waves, and spectrographs measure the chemical properties of objects in space.

In 1965, two astronomers designed a special radiometer. This led to the discovery that background microwave **radiation** was spreading throughout the universe. Most astronomers had theorized that if the Big Bang set off a huge, hot expansion, there would be leftover radiation everywhere in space. This turned out to be the case. Arno Penzia and Robert Woodrow Wilson are the physicists who discovered that background radiation. They won the Nobel Prize for Physics in 1978 for their discovery. The "snow" or static you see on your television when a station signal drops is background radiation from the Big Bang!

Indian astronomers using a telescope in Chile found support for another theory related to the Big Bang. Astronomers had predicted that older objects, which had formed right after the Big Bang, would be hotter than younger ones that formed later on. This, too, has turned out to be a fact.

In 2008, astronomers observed one of the oldest galaxies ever formed in images the Hubble Telescope sent back to Earth. The light from that galaxy took 13 billion years to reach Earth. The galaxy's light has the spectrum and chemical characteristics astronomers predicted objects would have if they formed shortly after the Big Bang.

Some mysteries about the Big Bang remain to be tested. However, repeated tests have solved many other mysteries.

OUR SOLAR SYSTEM

More than 8 billion years after the Big Bang—4.6 billion years ago—the birth of our solar system took place within the universe. Experts believe that the solar system, with our **Sun** at the center, probably developed in several stages.

An event, such as a supernova, caused a floating cloud of gases, dust, and ice in the spaces between stars to collapse. The collapse formed a spinning nebula made up of gases, space dust, and ice, which fell into the center of a disk. (A disk is a circular, flat area in space made up of dust and gas, and may

The Sun is the central star in our solar system and makes life on Earth possible. When sunlight hits someone lying on the beach, it has traveled 94.5 million miles (152 kilometers) in just eight minutes.

The Sun developed into a hot star long before any planets formed around it. Its solar heat melted away ice from Mercury, Mars, Earth, and Venus— the rocky inner planets.

include stars.) The collapse released energy, causing an early star to form and heat up at the center of the disk. That star would become the Sun.

As the Sun formed, it pushed out gases and dust. This leftover, pushed-out matter formed particles in the disk. Over time, collisions, gravity, and chemical changes took place within the disk. Material left over from the Sun's formation clustered together at different times and in different chemical combinations. Many astronomers believe that as clusters grew, gravity began to pull in more solar leftovers from the disk. These leftovers were made up of space dust, gas, and ice. Some of that dust clustered to form rocks and asteroids. Other matter combined to form Earth and other rocky terrestrial, or Earth-like planets, such as Venus, Mars, and Mercury. The giant gas planets, Jupiter and Saturn, were formed by gases in space. Uranus and Neptune were formed by ice.

Every object in the solar system is related chemically to every other object in the system. Therefore, studying the composition of other planets, such as Mercury, helps astronomers learn more about how our own planet Earth began.

WHAT MAKES A PLANET A PLANET?

These are changing times for planets. In 2006, astronomers came up with a new definition of a planet. The International Astronomical Union (IAU) defines a planet as "a **celestial** body that

- is in **orbit** around the Sun
- has sufficient **mass** for its self-gravity to overcome rigid body forces so that it assumes a hydrostatic equilibrium (nearly round) shape
- has cleared the neighborhood around its orbit."

This illustration shows the major planets and their positions in relation to each other and to the Sun.

Mercury (right) and Earth's Moon (left) are nearly the same size. But Mercury's distance from Earth makes it seem smaller than the Moon.

In other words, in addition to orbiting the Sun and being round, a planet has to be large enough so that its gravity or magnetism affects nearby stray objects and forces. In 2006, astronomers decided that Pluto did not fit the definition of planet. It was too small to influence any neighboring objects near it. With Pluto out of the "Big Eight" group of planets, is Mercury the next to go? Even though it is now the smallest planet in the solar system, Mercury is in no immediate danger of being booted out as a planet. Why? The center of Mercury, like Earth's, seems to be made up of a high percentage of circulating liquid, or molten, iron and nickel. Since Mercury is a planet rich in metals, it can influence everything around its orbit due to its magnetism. This ability to dominate nearby matter is a key characteristic that Pluto lacks. For a small planet, Mercury packs enough power to affect the solar winds the Sun gives off. So Mercury, despite its small size, is influential enough to be considered a full-fledged planet.

2

EARLY MERCURY DISCOVERIES

The nameless tomb lay hidden beneath the sands near Luxor, Egypt for more than three thousand years. No one in modern times knew of the tomb, for no records of it had ever been found. That changed in January 1927 when the archaeologist H. E. Winlock discovered something unexpected. Winlock was poking around a quarry from which ancient Egyptians had cut rocks for building projects. Behind a crumbling mud brick wall, Winlock found a tomb dedicated to an important royal advisor named Senenmut, who lived approximately 3,500 years ago. Within the chambers of Senenmut's tomb was the earliest known

This Egyptian tomb star ceiling (dated from around 1305 to 1290 BCE) shows the constellations at the top with scenes from everyday life in Ancient Egypt on the bottom. Early civilizations often connected human events with objects moving across the sky.

star ceiling. On the tomb's ceiling, ancient artists had carved images of objects in the skies. These included an unusually close lineup of the planets that were visible in 1534 BCE. One of those planets would eventually be called Mercury.

MERCURY BEFORE TELESCOPES

During Senenmut's time, just as now, Mercury was only visible to the eye—without the aid of telescopes or other tools—at dusk and at dawn and only at certain times of the year. Usually the Sun's glare, and the angle at which Mercury appears, make it difficult to see the planet regularly. Mercury's twice-a-day appearance was as unique to the Egyptians as its speediness in moving around the Sun. Despite the difficulty in seeing Mercury streak across the sky, someone living more than three thousand years ago had seen the planet and made sure it was recorded on the ancient star ceiling. The Senenmut tomb ceiling shows the earliest known image of Mercury, which is represented as a star. Recording the movement of the objects in the sky is an ancient practice that began even before the Egyptians of Senenmut's time. Throughout history, objects moving across the sky helped humans to measure time.

More than seven thousand years ago, ancient people settled down and began to raise animals and crops in fixed locations instead of traveling around to hunt and gather all the food they ate. From their communities, people began to notice that objects moved through the sky in predictable ways over a certain time period. These first settlers, who lived in what is now the Middle East, began to make connections between the passage of time

Ancient people sometimes believed that meteors were signs that a calamity—a flood or widespread disease—might be coming.

and the position of the Sun, the Moon, the stars, and other planets. Their movements helped farmers plan their growing seasons. Individuals who could read and write kept detailed records of what they saw night by night. Scientists and other researchers have discovered many celestial records and calendars all over the world in many forms.

The earliest settled people to keep extensive records of celestial events were the Sumerians, Babylonians, and Assyrians. They lived in the Middle East around 3,500 years ago. Their records influenced later astronomers in Egypt, Greece, Rome, China, and India, as well as early Jewish, Christian, and Muslim record keepers who developed their own calendar systems. In the Western hemisphere, Mayans living in what is now Central America also watched the skies and organized their lives with calendars. They noted Mercury's morning appearance in 733 BCE and its evening appearance in 727 BCE.

The regular appearances of objects in the sky gave ancient people a way to measure days, nights, and seasons on calendars such as this Mexican Sun calendar.

While calendar systems gave people practical information, the objects overhead inspired stories and beliefs in observers below. Early astronomers, and many later ones, also served their communities as religious figures. Many believed that the movement of the stars and planets were messages from heavenly gods to humans about events that had happened or would occur. This method of tying activity in the heavens to make predictions about human events is a belief system called astrology. Astronomy, on the other hand, is a science based on theoretical predictions that can be tested repeatedly with the same results. Ancient sky watchers used both astrology and astronomy to make sense of events in the sky and on Earth.

The Sumerians recorded their observations about the Sun, moon, stars, and planets on clay tablets. The early Babylonians who later occupied Sumerian lands continued to use clay tablets

Archaeologists who unearthed ancient clay tablets learned that ancient Sumerians described the planets as "children of the moon."

Early Greeks who observed the fastest orbiting planet named it Hermes, after the swift messenger god. The Romans adopted the same god and renamed him—and the planet—Mercury.

to record information about the sky. One tablet with lines from a famous Babylonian poem called the "Epic of Gilgamesh" mentions observations of the planet that would later be known as Mercury.

Like the Sumerians, the Babylonians understood that planets moved faster than stars. They thought of the visible planets—later named Jupiter, Venus, Saturn, Mars, and Mercury—as "stray sheep" since the planets appeared to move around. These early astronomers also named these planets after their gods, whom they believed lived in the stars and planets. Nabu or Nebo was the name they used for the planet we know as Mercury. Nabu or Nebo was a wise messenger to the gods. These early people probably thought of the planet as a messenger because they observed how quickly the planet moved around the Sun—in eighty-eight days. In comparison, Earth takes more than four times longer to orbit the Sun. These ancient planet gazers gave Mercury both a male and a female name because they thought of the planet as two objects that seemed to appear twice a day. The Greeks, like the Babylonians before them, gave the planet two names. Apollo was the Greeks' name for the morning planet, and Hermes was the name of the evening planet.

Around 400 BCE Eudoxus, a Greek astronomer, observed that the morning and evening appearances of Mercury took place at the same intervals. He realized the planet was a single object. The Greeks kept the name Hermes, which the Romans renamed Mercury. In 265 BCE, a Greek astronomer named Timocharis included Mercury in one of the earliest star catalogues.

Lacking telescopes for thousands of years, early astronomers relied on mathematics to make predictions about objects in the sky. Mercury was particularly hard to follow, but astronomers kept trying. Hundreds of years after Timocharis's death, astronomers developed mathematics sophisticated enough to make some predictions about when and where Mercury would appear in the sky.

TELESCOPIC CLOSE-UPS OF MERCURY

With the development of the telescope in the 1600s CE, astronomers made great progress in testing out their mathematical theories about Mercury and other celestial objects. One German astronomer, Johannes Kepler, calculated that Mercury would pass between the Sun and Earth at certain times and block a tiny part of the Sun's light. This passage, which looks like a spot on the Sun, is called a transit. Kepler, and later astronomers, recognized that objects transiting between the Sun and Earth were planets and not other objects. (Only transits by Mercury and Venus can be seen from Earth.)

Just thirteen Mercury transits take place in every hundred-year period. The transits occur only in May and November. That is the period when Mercury is in a viewable position from certain locations on Earth. And, of course, the weather must be clear. Unfortunately, Kepler, who pioneered discoveries in the motion of planets, died shortly before he could witness the Mercury transit he predicted would take place in 1630. Another astronomer at that time, Gassendi,

This page from Johannes Kepler's 1619 book, *The Harmony of the World*, shows the musical "tunes" that Kepler believed the planets made as they orbited in space.

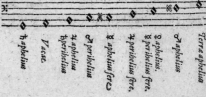

did see the transit Kepler had predicted. The most recent transit of Mercury took place on November 8, 2006. The next one will occur in 2016.

Nine years after Kepler died, an Italian astronomer named Zupus observed that Mercury had moonlike phases when the Sun hits the planet at different angles. As telescopes improved, astronomers began to see more features on all of the planets. In 1881, an Italian astronomer, Giovanni Schiaparelli, developed ways of viewing Mercury during the day since it cannot be seen from Earth at night. He made some drawings of the planet, though he was frustrated by his limited results. He noted canals on Mercury that others later thought were manmade. Schiaparelli theorized that the planet seemed to show the same side to the Sun because he thought that the Mercury day was the same length as the Mercury year.

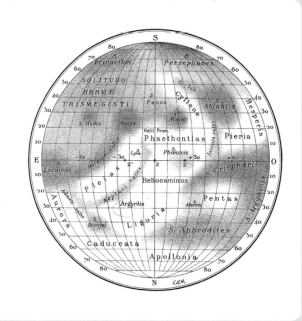

Astronomers used Eugene Antoniadi's Mercury maps and drawings for decades until new developments in telescopes brought Mercury into sharper focus.

A powerful telescope and a determined astronomer in France disproved some earlier theories about Mercury. From 1914 to 1929, Eugene Antoniadi studied Mercury with the help of a sophisticated telescope. Like Schiaparelli, Antoniadi also thought that one side of the planet always faced the Sun. However, he declared that the so-called manmade canals on Mercury were an illusion. His findings established that Mercury took the equivalent of eighty-eight Earth days to orbit the Sun. That is the length of Mercury's year. Like previous astronomers, Antoniadi assumed that Mercury also took eighty-eight Earth days to spin like a top on its Northern and Southern endpoints, or **axis**. He produced a detailed map of Mercury, complete with the names of the planet's features.

Radio Telescope

Nestled in the crater of a dead volcano and surrounded by tropical jungle thirty miles from the small city of Arecibo, Puerto Rico, is one of the world's most high-tech telescopes. The Arecibo Telescope has been positioned in the crater since 1963. Shortly after that, it began beaming **radar signals** out to objects in space. One of those objects was Mercury.

Soon the Arecibo Telescope began receiving reflected signals that bounced back from Mercury. This information showed that while Antoniadi had made several brilliant observations of Mercury, he and earlier astronomers were wrong about a few things. Mercury did not constantly face the Sun. The planet also did not take eighty-eight Earth days to rotate on its axis. It turns out that Mercury is both speedy and slow. It does orbit around the Sun in eighty-eight Earth days, making its year faster than an Earth-year. (A "year" is the time it takes a planet to orbit the Sun.) But Mercury is slow because it takes just a bit more than fifty-eight Earth days to spin on its axis. (A "day" is the time it takes a planet to completely rotate around its axis.) By comparison, Earth is a speed demon, taking only twenty-four hours to spin on its axis.

The powerful Arecibo Telescope has made many breakthrough discoveries within Earth's solar system. In the 1990s, astronomers at Arecibo first detected planets outside the solar system.

Comets, asteroids, or ancient planet gases may have deposited water on Mercury, which formed ice. The Sun's broiling rays do not reach the poles where the ice formed.

In the 1990s, astronomers viewing images of Mercury got a surprise. Mercury seems to have ice at its poles. These are the north and south endpoints of the axis on which Mercury rotates. How is it possible for ice to form on a planet that can get as hot as 700 degrees Fahrenheit (371 degrees Celsius)? One theory is that tall polar cliffs keep sections of Mercury's poles in shadows, and the sunlight never reaches those areas.

Between 2005 and 2006, astronomers learned something else about Mercury. Astronomers coordinated several Earth-based telescopes to measure slight variations in Mercury's spin rate. Such variations would show whether the planet's core was indeed made up of molten metal. In May, 2007, Jean-Luc Margot, a Cornell University researcher, reported this in *Science* magazine: "For a long time it was thought we'd have to land spacecraft on Mercury to learn if its core is solid or molten. Now we've answered that question using ground-based telescopes. The variations in Mercury's spin rate that we measured are best explained by a core that is at least partially molten. We have a 95 percent confidence level in this conclusion."

What other mysteries would astronomers solve when they no longer viewed the solar system's smallest planet using telescopes on the ground? Would astronomers prove or disprove earlier theories? What would astronomers and humankind learn when space-age technology left Earth to get a closer look at this amazing planet?

Scientists have discovered that Mercury is shrinking. As it cools down, its liquid iron core, which takes up 60 percent of its mass, is becoming solid. When the liquid becomes solid, the planet's size is reduced.

3
MERCURY IN THE
SPACE AGE

Mercury could no longer hide many of its secrets once more sophisticated telescopes, spacecraft, cameras, and computers went to work in space. On November 3, 1973, the National Aeronautics and Space Administration (NASA) launched the spacecraft *Mariner 10*. The mission was a "twofer." For the first time ever, a spacecraft used the gravity of one planet, Venus, to approach another one, Mercury. This slingshot approach saved fuel so that NASA could use a smaller, cheaper spacecraft for the mission.

Mariner 10's mission was to conduct several experiments as it orbited the planet. The equipment and tests included two cameras coordinated with onboard telescopes to televise the surface of Venus as well as nearly half of Mercury. Two spectrometers

Mercury, a hard-to-see planet for so many centuries, came into clear view when *Mariner 10* made its first approach in 1974.

Different parts of spacecraft are designed to perform specific tasks. Scientists and engineers spent years designing and building *Mariner 10*. Many of *Mariner 10*'s features were successfully adapted for other spacecraft.

were designed to measure Mercury's thin **atmosphere**. Two plasma detectors would measure energized solar particles that make up solar wind in space. The planet's magnetism would be measured by two magnetometers. A radiometer was included to measure Mercury's heat discharges. An onboard radio **telemetry** network would determine the length of Mercury's diameter and its mass.

From the start, NASA engineers were nervous about the *Mariner 10* mission. They only had about a one-month period to launch the spacecraft. That was the short amount of time when sunlight would provide enough contrast for astronomers to view Mercury's features. Problems developed early on with the craft's antennae and flight data systems on the way to Venus. Fortunately, engineers worked around the early problems. Three months and two days after takeoff from Cape Canaveral Air Force Station in Florida, *Mariner 10* flew by Venus. Onboard cameras took thousands of pictures of Venus on the way to Mercury.

But the major mission—approaching Mercury—was still ahead. Would the first ever slingshot gravity assist work? As planned, Venus's gravity gave *Mariner 10* a boost that sent the spacecraft toward Mercury. However, new problems developed as *Mariner 10* got closer to the Sun than any other spacecraft had before. NASA engineers had designed *Mariner 10* with many protections to deal with solar heat. Still, small flakes of *Mariner 10*'s coating began to peel off. Some of those flakes blocked one of the spacecraft's steering mechanisms. This, in turn, caused the craft to use up more fuel, which could cause the mission to fail.

NASA engineers used quick, creative thinking. They shifted *Mariner 10*'s solar panels to capture solar wind. This energy gave the spacecraft the power it the needed to continue its mission without using fuel at all. The "solar sailing" technique was a first. On later missions into space, NASA's designers would use this solar sailing technique to power other spacecraft and minimize fuel use. With the fuel problem solved, engineers positioned *Mariner 10* to fly by Mercury.

The planned experiments began on March 29, 1974. That day *Mariner 10* flew by Mercury just 437 miles (703 kilometers) away. Two more flybys took place. On September 21, 1974, from nearly 30,000 miles (48,069 km) away, *Mariner 10*'s cameras photographed the sunny side of the planet as well as its southern pole. A third flyby, just 203 miles (327 km) from the planet, took place on March 16, 1975.

During the three flybys, *Mariner 10* took more than ten thousands pictures of Mercury. From these, NASA scientists mapped more than half of the planet's features, filling in details

Mariner 10 was the last of the *Mariner* missions. But it was the first spacecraft to explore Mercury, to use solar sailing to save fuel, and to employ gravity from one planet to get to another.

earlier astronomers only imagined. *Mariner 10* successfully completed its mission and unlocked many secrets about Mercury's nearly 5-billion-year history.

After *Mariner 10*'s fuel was gone, NASA instructed the spacecraft to turn itself off. Though blind, it is still in orbit. Its cameras and telescopes can no longer view Mercury nor send back more information. Both the planet and the spacecraft orbit the Sun in silence. But before *Mariner 10* went dead, it gave scientists more information than earlier astronomers could have ever hoped for. At the end of the mission, NASA had thousands of close-up images filled with details describing Mercury's appearance—its shape and surface, its atmosphere, its temperature and mass, and its behavior as it orbited the Sun.

This March, 1974 mosaic of images (a combination of Mercury photographs arranged to show the whole planet) shows Mercury's surface before *Mariner 10* left the planet's neighborhood for good.

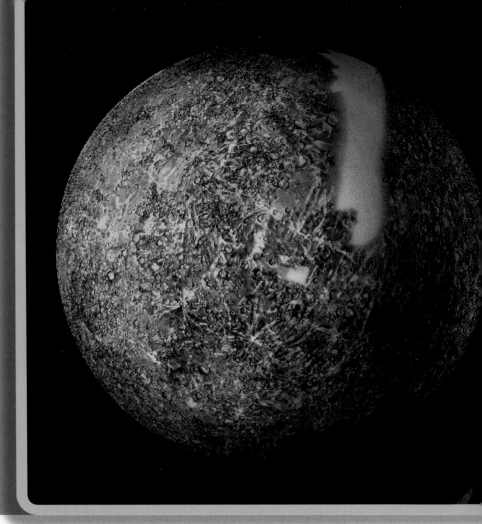

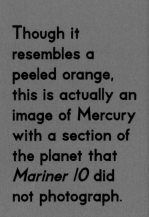

Though it resembles a peeled orange, this is actually an image of Mercury with a section of the planet that *Mariner 10* did not photograph.

MERCURY'S SHAPE

Mariner 10's coordinated television cameras and telescopes showed a rounder planet than scientists had expected. Mercury is almost a perfect sphere. Measurements around its equator are almost the same as the measurements between its northern and southern poles, or endpoints. Earth's measurements do not form such a perfect sphere. Images did not reveal any related natural **satellites**, such as moons, orbiting Mercury.

MERCURY'S ATMOSPHERE

Mariner 10's spectrometers measured Mercury's atmosphere and made an important discovery. The planet has practically no atmosphere. Atmosphere is a layer of gases that surrounds a planet. Over billions of years, a planet undergoes changes that release gases into the atmosphere. Volcanoes may spew gases. When rocks wear away, they release chemicals that affect the atmosphere. Objects hitting a planet cause atmospheric changes. Temperature changes also affect a planet and cause it to release gases. *Mariner 10* found that Mercury's wisps of atmosphere were made up of barely measurable quantities of helium and hydrogen. The planet's location so close to the Sun is one reason for Mercury's thin atmosphere. Strong solar winds long ago destroyed the gases that Mercury gave off as it formed. While Mercury's magnetism affects nearby objects, its gravity is too weak to hold onto atmospheric gases. As a result, the gases float off into space.

Without atmosphere to protect the planet like a blanket, life on Mercury is impossible. Also, without much atmosphere, the planet has long been exposed to the bombardment of comets and asteroids flying through space. There is not enough atmosphere to scatter sunlight or the light from other stars. The sky over Mercury is nearly black. And there is not enough atmospheric pressure to help sound waves travel. Mercury's lack of significant atmosphere makes it a silent place.

MERCURY'S SURFACE

Mariner 10's three flybys produced close-up photos of Mercury. They showed a planet marked with moonlike craters, plains, and cliffs over its visible surface. This told NASA scientists that asteroids and other objects in space had smashed into the planet in its early life. One particular impact crater, called the Caloris Basin, is one of the largest craters ever seen in the solar system. Caloris means "heat" in Latin. When the Sun hits the crater, temperatures can build up to more than 700 degrees Fahrenheit (371 degrees C).

Imagine what the Caloris Basin bombardment must have looked like. A fiery asteroid about the width of Connecticut streaked tens of thousands of miles per hour through space. It smashed into Mercury with such force that it created a crater the approximate size of Texas. Not only that, but the impact pushed up nearly mile-high mountains around the crater

Most asteroid and meteor impacts on Mercury's surface probably took place during the Heavy Bombardment, which was a distant period billions of years ago when all the planets formed.

WHAT'S IN A MERCURY NAME?

Once astronomers could get a closer look at the planet, they needed names for Mercury's craters, ridges, hills, and plains. The International Astronomical Union came up with a naming system for Mercury's visible features. The IAU will continue to use this system when current and future missions map new features on Mercury.

Craters are named after artists from around the world—authors, painters, sculptors, and musicians. (The Caloris Basin is an exception. It was named before the IAU developed the Mercury feature-naming system.) Examples include Bach Crater, Bronte Crater, Dickens Crater, Hiroshige Crater, Homer Crater, Li Po Crater, Rodin Crater, Sarmiento Crater, and Turgenev Crater.

Planitia, or plains, are named after a country's name for Mercury. Examples of these names include Budh Planitia (Indian), Suisei Planitia (Japanese), and Tir Planitia (Norse).

Rupes, the cliffs on Mercury, are named after ships used in explorations. Adventure Rupe, Astrolabe Rupe, Discovery Rupe, Endeavor Rupe, Santa Maria Rupe are names of some of Mercury's cliffs.

Each *dorsum*, or ridge, is named after astronomers who have studied Mercury, such as Antoniadi Dorsum and Schiaparelli Dorsum. The *vallis*, or valleys, on Mercury are named after some of the major telescopes used to view Mercury. For example, Arecibo Vallis, Goldstone Vallis, Haystack Vallis, and Simeiz Vallis are all names of some of Mercury's valleys.

The Haystack Observatory is located in Massachusetts.

rim. The crash also sent shock waves right through, or possibly around the planet, to the other side. This caused ragged hills to rise up in the area directly opposite from the impact.

However, Mercury is not just made up of craters. Just like the other terrestrial rocky planets like Mars, Venus, and Earth, Mercury has smooth areas. Heavy volcanic activity in Mercury's distant past caused lava flows and falling ash that cooled to form smooth plains.

Before explorations of Mercury occurred, scientists could only guess what the planet's surface looked like. However, recent explorations of Mercury have helped to paint a clearer picture.

Mercury is wrinkled as well as jagged and smooth. When Mercury's core cooled after its formation, the surface shrunk and formed wrinkles. These wrinkles are in the form of upward curving cliffs called rupes (Latin for "cliff"). One cliff, the Discovery Rupe, is nearly a mile high (15 km).

MERCURY'S MAGNETISM

Mariner 10 had magnometers protected by sunshades and thermal blankets. They showed that the planet had an unexpected magnetic field. Scientists learned this because *Mariner 10*'s plasma detectors measured disturbances in solar wind around the planet. That meant a magnetic field on Mercury's surface was strong enough to cause changes in the solar field. This is surprising since Mercury is a small planet. (Earth's magnetic field is one hundred times stronger and keeps solar wind away from the planet.) An iron core inside a planet conducts electrical current that affects other objects nearby. It turns out that Mercury's core takes up a whopping 75 percent of its diameter—2,250 miles (3,621 km) deep from Mercury's center to its rocky crust. This would account for its unexpected magnetic field.

NASA scientists wondered how a small planet, which should have cooled off by now, could still contain such a large, hot, iron core. *Mariner 10* was not equipped to explain that puzzle in 1974. However, NASA engineers put questions about Mercury's surprising magnetism on its "to do" list for future missions to Mercury.

MERCURY'S MASS

Although Mercury is a small planet, it is dense. (Density is a measurement of how heavy an object is in terms of the amount of space it takes up.) Only Earth's matter is denser—eighteen to twenty times more dense. The radio telemetry system onboard *Mariner 10* discovered Mercury's density by measuring how much of Mercury's gravity affected the spacecraft as it orbited Mercury.

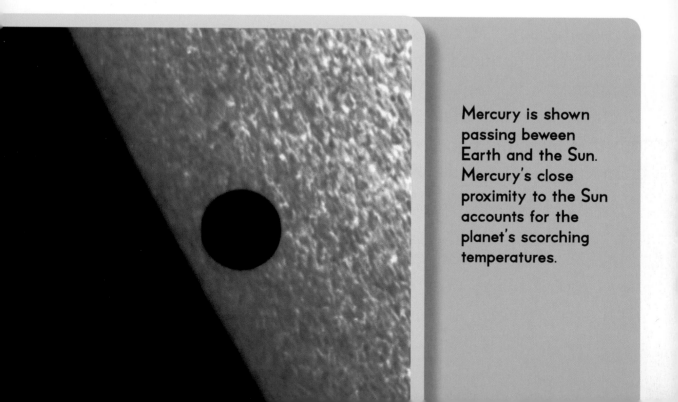

Mercury is shown passing beween Earth and the Sun. Mercury's close proximity to the Sun accounts for the planet's scorching temperatures.

MERCURY'S TEMPERATURE

Of all the planets, Mercury has the greatest temperature contrasts. Scientists learned from the radiometer readings that Mercury is a planet of temperature extremes. Orbiting so close to the Sun means that during its "sunny daytime," which lasts about fifty-nine Earth days, temperatures can reach more than 700 degrees Fahrenheit (371 degrees C). But in darkness, also fifty-nine Earth days, Mercury's temperature plunges to about -300 degrees Fahrenheit or so (-180 degrees C.)

MERCURY'S ORBIT

For decades early in the twentieth century, astronomers believed that a hidden planet existed closer to the Sun than

All the Sun's planets formed over time after the Big Bang, yet each has its own shape, composition, and orbit.

	MERCURY	**EARTH**
DIAMETER	3,100 miles (4,900 km)	7,926 miles (12,756 km
DISTANCE FROM SUN	About 36 million miles (58 million km)	About 93 million miles (150 million
ATMOSPHERE	thin	thick
AVERAGE TEMPERATURE RANGE	Mercury can be six to ten times hotter than Earth	
DAYTIME	750 degrees Fahrenheit (400 degrees C)	75 degrees Fahrenheit (20 degrees C)
NIGHTTIME	-330 degrees Fahrenheit (-200 degrees C)	40 degrees Fahrenheit (10 degrees C)
LENGTH OF DAY	176 Earth days	24 hours
LENGTH OF YEAR	88 Earth days	365 days
FORCE OF GRAVITY	One-third of Earth's gravity	
SOLAR WIND	Solar particles actually land on Mercury because its atmosphere is too thin to keep them out.	Earth's atmosphere protects the planet from solar particl
POSSIBILITY OF LIFE	No life possible	Life exists
LARGEST CRATER	Caloris Basin 900 miles (1,500 km)	Vredefort, South Africa 87 miles (300 km)

Mercury. Something was causing oddities in Mercury's orbit that mathematics could not explain. The astronomers wondered if a planet they could not see was the cause. They named the unseen planet Vulcan.

Mercury's orbit is elliptical, or egg-shaped, just as the orbits of most of the other planets are. However, Mercury's egg-shaped orbit is particularly long. This unusual shape means that if it were possible to stand in certain locations on Mercury, sunrises and sunsets would look very bizarre. The sun would be seen as rising part way, then stopping, then suddenly reversing.

Mercury's orbit has another oddity. In part of its orbit, Mercury moves faster than astronomers once predicted. Picture a small marble orbiting a large marble in the center of a thin floating sheet of rubber. The weight of the large marble will create a slope that causes gravity to pull down at the small marble and its orbit. The small marble then picks up speed slightly before heading out of the slope and bringing its orbit with it.

In a similar way, out in space, the Sun's heavy mass warps the space in which Mercury travels as well as the planet's orbit. It is not Planet Vulcan, but warped space and gravity, which cause Mercury's wobble and acceleration. The physicist Albert Einstein had predicted Mercury's orbital acceleration. He described the physics involved in his General Theory of Relativity, which he published in 1915. Einstein's theory has been proven repeatedly ever since.

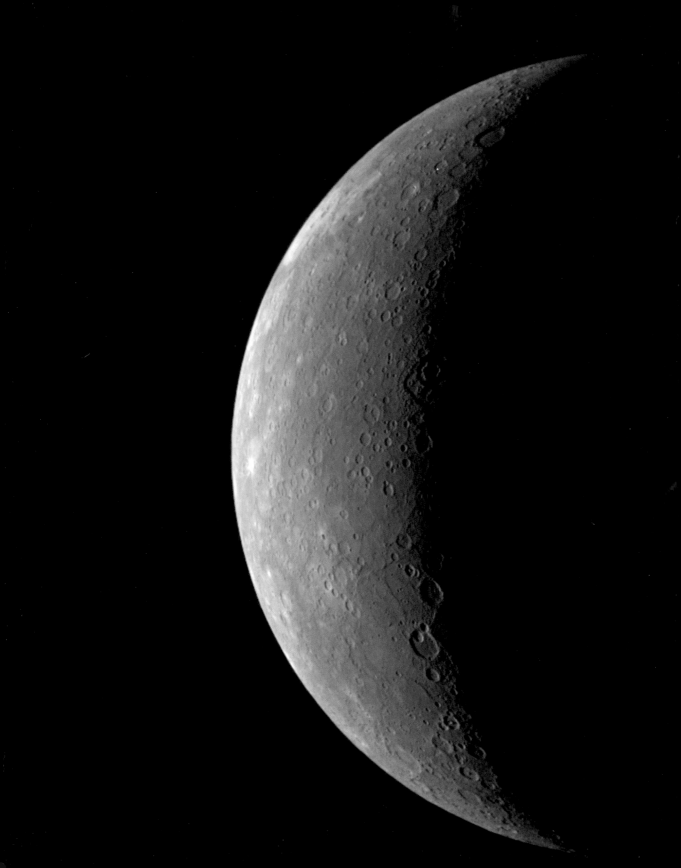

4
PRESENT AND FUTURE MERCURY MISSIONS

After *Mariner 10*'s spectacular performance in the 1970s, scientists wanted to learn more. NASA decided it was time to study Mercury again. What would another visit to Mercury with the latest technology tell us about the planet and the origins of our solar system? On August 3, 2004, NASA launched the spacecraft *MESSENGER* to answer those questions. *MESSENGER* stands for **ME**rcury, **S**urface, **S**pace **EN**vironment, **GE**ochemistry and **R**anging). Seeking answers from the smallest planet in the solar system, NASA designed the spacecraft *MESSENGER* to answer the following questions:

- Why is Mercury so dense?
- What is Mercury's **geologic** history?
- What is the nature of Mercury's magnetic field?
- What is the structure of Mercury's core?

Mercury is the oldest, smallest, fastest, most dense planet in the solar system.

- What is the reflective material at Mercury's poles? If it is ice, did it come from comets or from within the planet in its past?
- What is the chemical composition of Mercury's atmosphere?

THE AMAZING *MESSENGER*

When you think of a spacecraft, do you picture something the size of a jumbo jet? Well, NASA's designers say *MESSENGER's* parts—its payload—would fit into an SUV vehicle. And, at 2441 pounds (1,107 kilograms) *MESSENGER* weighs about the same as a compact car. Miniaturized, lighter equipment that can be partially powered by the Sun cuts down on weight and the quantity of fuel needed by the spacecraft. That makes new spacecraft even more economical than ever before.

The many teams of scientists who worked on *MESSENGER* from Earth included physicists, geologists, chemists, aviation experts, engineers, and many other workers.

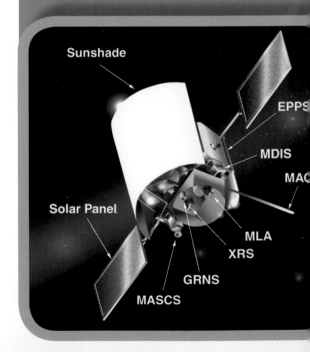

The economical *MESSENGER* cost about the same in today's dollars—around $450 million—as *Mariner 10* did thirty years ago.

Sunshade

EPPS

MDIS

MAC

Solar Panel

MLA

XRS

GRNS

MASCS

The Johns Hopkins University Applied Physics Laboratory (APL) in Laurel, Maryland, designed and built *MESSENGER*. APL controls the mission for NASA and coordinates operations with several other institutions in the United States and around the world. Specialists take shifts communicating with *MESSENGER* from Deep Space Stations in the Mojave Desert in California, Spain, and Australia.

Although Mercury's neighborhood is hot, *MESSENGER* is cool. Its designers came up with strong, lightweight materials that resist the scorching heat of the Sun. Fortunately, another design feature keeps the *MESSENGER* cool—its ceramic fabric sunshade, which is about 8 by 6 feet (2 by 2.5 m) tall. When the spacecraft is closest to the Sun, the front of the sunshade may heat up to 700 degrees Fahrenheit (371 degrees C). But the back of it only reaches room temperature—about 70 degrees Fahrenheit (20 degrees C). A system of pipes and insulation around the craft also protects *MESSENGER* from burning up. The delicate instruments performing the mission's tests are also protected from the burning heat. One of them is suspended by special strings in a Thermos-like container inside a refrigerator that keeps it cool.

Two solar panels and two batteries work together to use sunlight to power the spacecraft's ordinary energy needs— operating the sunshades and solar shield, working the testing instruments, and providing power to the communications network. The onboard fuel will mainly be used to slow down the spacecraft when it enters Mercury's orbit in 2011. Fuel takes up 54 percent of *MESSENGER's* weight. The craft will need that fuel power to fight against the Sun's gravity that would otherwise speed it up too fast.

MESSENGER's seven measuring and testing instruments were miniaturized to fit behind the sunshade so they would not block views of Mercury. These instruments could not weigh more than 110 pounds (50 kg), the size of a small person. *MESSENGER's* instruments include

- Wide- and narrow-angle cameras to take pictures of Venus and Mercury
- Plasma and particle spectrometers to measure Mercury's magnetosphere
- Magnetometer to map Mercury's magnetic field
- X-ray, gamma-ray and neutron spectrometers to detect elements on Mercury's surface and its crust
- Laser altimeter to map Mercury's terrain
- Atmospheric and surface composition spectrometer to measure atmosphere and surface composition

LAUNCHING *MESSENGER*

Spacecraft like *MESSENGER* are launched with rockets and then released into space. When Delta II rockets lifted off with *MESSENGER* at dawn on August 3, 2004, from the Cape Canaveral

Air Force Station in Florida, the spacecraft left Earth forever. Its six-and-a-half-year journey would cover 4.9 million miles (7.9 million km) to reach Mercury's orbit in 2011. Scientists had learned a lot since *Mariner 10* when the idea of a slingshot gravity assist was brand new. By 2007, several NASA spacecraft had used the maneuver successfully. As planned, *MESSENGER* made a flyby over Earth and two over Venus, where a gravity assist sent it toward Mercury.

Venus's gravity assist worked smoothly to slow down the spacecraft as it headed toward Mercury and the Sun's gravity. While they had the spacecraft in Venus's neighborhood, engineers on Earth adjusted instruments, performed some tests on Venus's atmosphere, and photographed the planet as it traveled nearby. Seven months later, on January 14, 2008, *MESSENGER* performed its first Mercury flyby and began its many tests.

NASA scheduled seven *MESSENGER* flybys over Earth, Venus, and Mercury when it launched on August 3, 2004. As of October 6, 2008, the spacecraft successfully accomplished five of them.

WHERE IS MESSENGER?

August 3, 2004: Launch from Cape
Canaveral Air Force Station in Florida

August 2, 2005: Flyby above Earth at an
altitude of 1,458 miles (2,348 km)

October 24, 2006: Flyby above Venus at
an altitude of 1,856 miles (2,987 km)

June 5, 2007: Second flyby above Venus
at an altitude of 210 miles (338 km)

January 14, 2008: Flyby above Mercury
at an altitude of 200 miles (2,348 km)

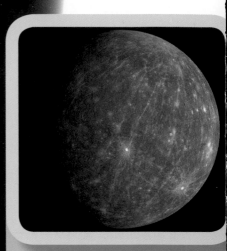

October 6, 2008: Second flyby above
Mercury at an altitude of 200 miles
(2,348 km)

Each *MESSENGER*
flyby has given scientists
more information about
Mercury. *MESSENGER's*
October 6, 2008 flyby
photographed several
young craters on the
planet's surface that
scientists had not seen
before.

September 29, 2009: Third flyby above
Mercury at an altitude of 200 miles
(2,348 km)

March 18, 2011: *MESSENGER* will
disappear forever into Mercury's orbit.

A NEW OLD PLANET

When *MESSENGER* performed its first Mercury flyby and returned images and data, scientists on Earth were excited. One scientist who had worked on the *Mariner 10* mission, Bob Strom, said: "I was thinking in my mind that I'd see features like *Mariner 10* saw, but I was astounded at the quality of these images, and, after looking at them, it dawned on me that this is a whole new planet we're looking at. Every part of this planet, 'seen' or 'unseen,' is new."

MESSENGER's January 2008 flyby photographed Mercury's never-before-seen "spider crater" with more than one hundred radiating arms.

MERCURY

One "new" old feature was the Caloris Basin. Unlike *Mariner 10*, *MESSENGER* was able to get a complete view of the Texas-sized crater. Its size had been estimated at 810 miles (1,300 km). The crater turned out to be 960 miles across (1,500 km). While counting smaller craters within the Caloris Basin, scientists noticed there were fewer of them on one side. "That shows that there has been a lot of volcanic activity on Mercury," Strom said. In other words, volcanoes probably deposited ash and lava after the huge collision that formed the crater. Scientists also found something truly strange. Close to the center of the Caloris Basin, *MESSENGER* instruments photographed a spidery cluster about 25 miles (40 km) across. Geologists are discussing many theories about what may have caused this unusual feature.

Mercury's colors also surprised scientists who will be analyzing the kinds of geological activities that might have caused them. To the naked eye, Mercury appears gray. However, scientists have added color-enhanced images to views of Mercury to show colors that are only visible close-up.

The sun was shining on Mercury's enormous Caloris Basin during *MESSENGER*'s January 2008 flyby. This mission revealed that the Caloris was filled smaller, ringed craters, which scientists continue to study.

The International Astronomical Union (IAU) approved new names for the many features *MESSENGER* discovered and mapped during the January 8, 2008 flyby.

Magnometers measured Mercury's magnetic field and found its strength to be about the same as it was when *Mariner 10* visited. However, there were surprises, too. One scientist, Sean Solomon, said: "This tiny magnetosphere is full of hot plasma, some of it from the Sun, some of it from interactions between the surface and the atmosphere."

At the same time, unlike *Mariner 10*, *MESSENGER's* particle spectrometer did not observe any solar energy particles on Mercury. Solomon's reaction? "I think that tells us that the magnetosphere of Mercury is very changeable. It's a function of the [activity in the] atmosphere of the Sun; we went by at a particularly quiet period of solar activity, and [we think] it can change in a matter of minutes or hours. To prove that, we'll have to wait for some of the future observations we make during flybys." New observations were made during the October 2008 flyby and will continue in 2011 when *MESSENGER* enters Mercury's orbit.

BepiColombo

In 2019, Mercury's neighborhood is going to get another visitor. That is the approximate date when the *BepiColombo* spacecraft will enter Mercury's orbit after a voyage that is scheduled for 2013. Scientists from the European Space Agency and the Japanese Aerospace Exploration Agency developed *BepiColombo* to carry out further tests on Mercury's atmosphere, geology, and features. The space-craft has three parts that will be launched in one package. The journey to Mercury will take six years and will include a moon fly-by. Unfortunately, an actual landing on Mercury has been can-celled due to budgetary problems.

The spacecraft got its name from scientists who wanted to honor a beloved mathematician and engineer, Guiseppe Colombo (nicknamed Beppi) who lived from 1920 to 1984. Colombo was the engineer who first thought of the idea of using the gravity of one planet to get to another.

One of *BepiColombo*'s orbiters will map Mercury, and the second one will measure magnetism.

After the last photos that *MESSENGER* and *Bepi-Colombo* will take, people on Earth will have more knowledge than ever of its smaller neighbor, Mercury.

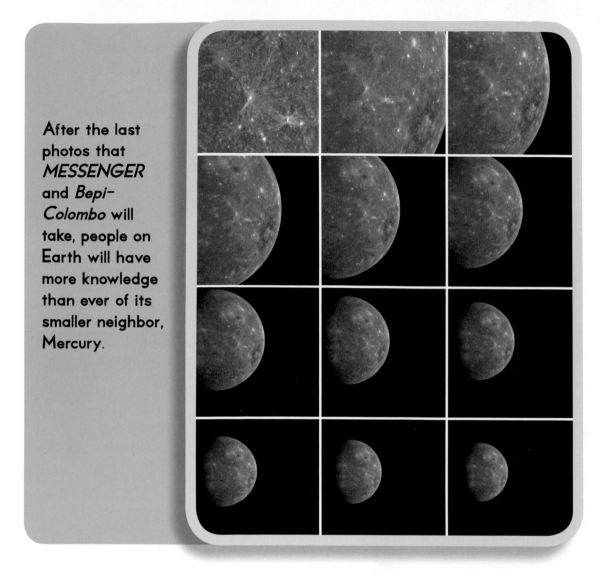

Mercury has turned out to be much more than what the astronomers once noted on the Senenmut star ceiling thousands of years ago in Egypt. Close-up images, computer data, and measurements have told the world a lot about this planet that formed so many billions of years ago. As more missions to Mercury are undertaken, we will learn more fascinating information about this small planet closest to the Sun.

QUICK FACTS
ABOUT MERCURY

NAME AND ORIGIN OR SOURCE OF NAME:
Mercury, Roman messenger to the gods

FIRST OR EARLY OBSERVATIONS OF THE PLANET:
Sumerian, Assyrian, Babylonian observations, approximately 1500 BCE;
Mayans: 733-727 BCE
Greek: 400 BCE Eudoxus;
265 BCE Timocharis

SIZE: 3,100 miles (4,900 km) in diameter

DISTANCE FROM EARTH: 48 million miles (77.3 million km)

DISTANCE FROM SUN: 28.6 million miles (46 million km)

NUMBER OF MOONS: No moons

TYPE OF PLANET: Terrestrial

TEMPERATURE RANGE: -330 degrees Fahrenheit (-200 degrees C)
to 750 degrees Fahrenheit (400 degrees C)

LENGTH OF A SOLAR DAY (from noon to noon): 176 Earth days

LENGTH OF YEAR (one orbit around the Sun): 88 Earth days

GLOSSARY

asteroid—A rocky object orbiting in space that may range in size from a few feet wide to hundreds of miles wide.

astronomer—A scientist who studies objects in space.

astronomy—The scientific study of objects in the universe.

atmosphere—The layer of gases that surround a planet.

axis—An imaginary straight line around which a celestial body spins.

celestial—Relating to the sky or outer space.

galaxy—A part of the universe made up of gases and millions of stars.

geology—The study of the rocks and the physical history of a planet.

mass—The amount of matter that makes up an object.

moon—A natural celestial object that orbits a planet and reflects light from a star.

orbit—The path a celestial body takes around another celestial body. An example is the path a planet takes as it goes around the Sun.

planet—A rocky, icy, or gaseous body that rotates around the Sun while influencing other nearby matter.

radar signals—Invisible radio waves that are used to calculate location and sometimes speed of objects.

radiation—Energy that gives off light waves or particles.

satellite—A natural or manmade object that orbits another object in space.

solar system—All the asteroids, comets, moons, and planets that move around the Sun.

star—A gaseous object in the sky that gives off light.

Sun—The heat- and light-producing star at the center of the solar system around which planets and other matter rotate.

telemetry—Electronic measurements and specific data.

universe—The space that contains all existing matter and energy.

FIND OUT MORE

BOOKS

Birch, Robin. *Mercury*. New York: Chelsea Clubhouse, 2008.

Loewen, Nancy. *Nearest to the Sun: The Planet Mercury*. Mankato, MN: Picture Window Books, 2008.

Oxlade, Chris. *Mercury, Mars, and Other Inner Planets*. New York: Rosen Central, 2008.

Parsons, Jayne, ed. *The Way the Universe Works*. New York: DK Children, 2006.

Perricone, Mike. *The Big Bang*. New York: Chelsea House, 2008.

Stille, Darlene. *Mercury*. Mankato, MN: Childs World, 2004.

World Book, Inc. *Mercury and Venus*. Chicago: World Book, 2007.

WEBSITES

BEPI-COLOMBO
http://sci.esa.int/science-e/www/area/index.cfm?fareaid=30

Discovery Mission: MESSENGER
http://discovery.nasa.gov/messenger.html

Exploring the Planet Mercury
http://www.spacetoday.org/SolSys/Mercury/MercuryResources.html

Mariner 10
http://nssdc.gsfc.nasa.gov/nmc/masterCatalog.do?sc=1973-085A

Mercury
http://stardate.org/resources/ssguide/mercury.html

Mercury: The Elusive Planet
http://btc.montana.edu/messenger/elusive_planet/elus_index.htm

MESSENGER: The Extreme Machine
http://www.nasa.gov/missions/solarsystem/f_messenger-extreme.html

The MESSENGER Mission
http://messenger.jhuapl.edu/the_mission/index.html

Starchild: The Planet Mercury
http://starchild.gsfc.nasa.gov/docs/StarChild/solar_system_level2/mercury.html

A Ten Step Program for Star and Planet Formation
http://cfa-www.harvard.edu/COMPLETE/learn/star_and_planet_formation.html

Understanding Mercury
http://www.nasm.si.edu/research/ceps/research/mercury/mercury.cfm

UNIVERSE 101: The Big Bang Theory
http://map.gsfc.nasa.gov/universe/bb_theory.html

Welcome to the Planets: Mercury
http://pds.jpl.nasa.gov/planets/choices/mercury1.htm

BIBLIOGRAPHY

The author found these resources especially helpful when researching this book.

Arnett, Bill. "Mercury." http://www.nineplanets.org/mercury.html

Astronomical Society of the Pacific. "Universe in the Classroom."
http://www.astrosociety.org/education/publications/tnl/22/22.html

Bond, Peter. *Distant Worlds: Milestones in Planetary Exploration*. New York:
Copernicus: in association with Praxis Publishing, Ltd., 2007.

Corfield, Richard, *Lives of the Planets: A Natural History of the Solar System*.
New York: Basic Books, 2007.

Dominique, Deborah, and C.T. Russell, *MESSENGER Mission to Mercury*. New
York: Springer Business Media, 2007.

Johns Hopkins University/Applied Physics Laboratory. "MESSENGER News
Center."
http://www.messengerjhuapl.edu/news_room/impressions_01_15_08.html

---. "Mercury and Ancient Cultures." http://btc.montana.edu/messenger/elusive_planet/ancient_cultures.php

Kluger, Jeffrey. "The Hot Rock: Mysterious Mercury, the Planet Closest to the Sun." Space. August 9, 2004.

Leary, Warren E. "Pictures Reveal Mercury's Tumultuous Past." *New York Times*, January 31, 2008. http://www.nytimes.com/2008/01/31/science/31mercury.html?ref=todayspaper

Moore, Patrick, *Moore on Mercury: The Planet and the Mission*. London: Springer-Verlag, 2007.

NASA. "Mercury." http://nssdc.gsfc.nasa.gov/planetary/planets/mercurypage.html

---. "Mercury, Get Ready for a Close-Up." http://www.nasa.gov/mission_pages/messenger/main/f_closeup.html

Novakovic, Bojan. "Senenmut: An Ancient Egyptian Astronomer." http://www.arxiv.org/pdf/0801.1331

Sobel, Dava. *The Planets*. New York: Viking, 2005 and 2007.

---. "Making mercury." *Science News*. April 15, 2006.

Small, Lawrence. "Being There: Robotic Spacecraft Allow Geologists to Explore Other Planets as if They Were On-site." *Smithsonian*. December, 2004.

---. "First Rock From the Sun." Planetary Science. *The Economist*. July 24, 2004.

---. "Scientists Gear Up For Mercury Mission Flyby Of Venus." *Science Daily*. June 5, 2007.

UC Davis. "Earliest Stage of Planet Formation Dated." http://www.news.ucdavis.edu/search/news_detail.lasso?id=8468

INDEX

Page numbers in **boldface** indicate
   photos or illustrations.

ABOUT THE AUTHOR

L.H. Colligan writes about many topics, from study skills to activity books to children's fiction and non-fiction on health and science topics. She lives in the Hudson Valley in New York. She has viewed the skies from her telescope, and one day hopes to see Mercury.